14 Days *of* Foreplay

USING PLAY TO INCREASE INTIMACY, CONNECTION, AND SUSTAINABILITY

MONICA LIESER

&

TIANNA ROONEY

ISBN: 1492746177
ISBN 13: 9781492746171
Library of Congress Control Number: 2013917209
CreateSpace Independent Publishing Platform, North Charleston, SC

Justin and Todd,
With the two of you as our team mates for life,
we are guaranteed to win.

We give a sincere thank you to all of the couples who have
trusted us through the years. Your willingness to take
risks, demonstrate vulnerability and to be playful is a true
gift. Your work has made our book possible.

Acknowledgements

Thank you Debi for sharing so generously of your talents. You helped a couple of therapists sound like writers. We are grateful. There are beautiful roads ahead for you.

Thank you Amy for showering us with your creativity through photography and design. And thank you for your patience with a few thousand feathers!

Anyone can be passionate, but it takes real lovers
to be silly.
– *Rose Franken, writer*

Meet *the* Playmakers

There are two parts of our lives that encouraged us to write this book. First and foremost, we are in happy and healthy (most of the time) marriages. Monica has been married for twelve years, and Tianna has been married for fifteen years. Our husbands are our best friends. We are grateful to be living our own marriages with intention and to have partners who dare to be married to marriage therapists. Can you imagine the pressure? Thankfully our partners are invested in "gestures of intention" even when this does not come naturally.

The second part of our lives that fed the content of this book is our careers. We are both licensed marriage and family therapists. We met during graduate school internship and felt a great connection to one another. Soon we realized that we see relationships through much the same lens. We went on to independently own group private practices, supervise other marriage and family therapists, teach at universities and have each served as President of our state professional associations.

Every day, we are gifted with couples inviting us to support their relationships. Thousands of hours of working with couples and learning from them as they find

"Laughing with my husband turns me on and my smile turns him on. For us, there is nothing sexier than playing creatively and often."
– Monica

"My hubby is the real author of this book. I'm kidding. But he is really good at foreplay and he continues to teach me to be my best in and out of the bedroom"
- Tianna

the courage to invest in one another is nothing short of inspiring.

We believe that *14 Days of Foreplay* gives our readers all the best of what we see to be effective in creating and sustaining healthy, playful, and long-lasting relationships.

Couples experience ebbs and flows in relationship satisfaction. It is no secret that remaining connected to your partner takes thoughtfulness and energy. This investment in your relationship doesn't have to *feel* like work. In fact, it can be fun and playful. This book teaches these gestures of intention through fourteen thought provoking, experiential, and intimate activities. If you are eager to ignite connection, be playful, take risks, and grow, then wrap yourself up in *14 Days of Foreplay*, and read on!

The Lingo

The payoffs are tremendous if both partners can commit to gestures of intention. We are of the mindset that using gestures of intention is a powerful way of communicating love, desire, and attraction. By gestures of intention, we are referring to intentional movements and behaviors that align with the goal of sending messages of tenderness and love.

For instance, a gesture of intention could be leaving the porch light on for your spouse when you know she or he has a late night at work. Another example may be asking how your spouse's important meeting went with his/her employer or even knowing that this important meeting was scheduled in the first place. Validation is perhaps the simplest, most powerful and effective form of a gesture of intention. Validation is the act of communicating that you have heard what a person has said and that you acknowledge the feelings and experience of the speaker.

We believe that activating fun and playful gestures of intention will bring a couple closer together in

> Gestures of intention: intentional movements and behaviors that align with the goal of sending messages of tenderness and love.

meaningful ways. The hard work is done; we have created the structure. Now all you and your partner have to do is follow directions. Our goal has been to keep this program simple, user-friendly, and fun.

The foundation of this program is based on the idea of **intimacy**. Intimacy is a term that most people see as synonymous with sex. Not the case. Sex is great and fun; however, intimacy is better. Intimacy makes sex *amazing*. Intimacy is an emotional and physical concept that represents the layers of a relationship. The more layers there are, the deeper the connectedness and the greater the intimacy. A basic way to understand intimacy is to break the word down: "Into Me See." Intimacy includes feelings of vulnerability soothed with trust. Members of a couple high on the intimacy scale would be willing to "be themselves" around each other and not fear judgment or other negative consequences such as abandonment.

> Intimacy includes feelings of vulnerability soothed with trust.

The structure of *14 Days* involves a series of intentional activities. Each activity is divided into three sections. First, the couple is taken through a **Stripping Down** section where background information is provided that supports the activity. "Stripping down" may include educational information and research to create a framework and rationale for the activity. It is a place to set the stage for the activity. **Doing It** is the instructional section that takes couples step-by-step through the activity. It is designed for you and your partner to connect in new and different ways. Finally, the **Afterglow** guides both partners through a reflection process. It includes questions to process back and forth as well as encouragements for journaling significant thoughts and feelings following the experience. We have provided space in the book for journaling. If you find that journaling is a barrier to sharing, because talking feels more comfortable, by all means, abandon the journaling.

The activities are sequentially ordered in an intentional fashion. It is recommended that you progress through the activities in order from one to fourteen (no skipping or breaking rules—yet). Your *14 Days* can be completed in any amount of time that works for your relationship. The sequence of activities has been carefully crafted to deliver powerful effects on a couple that ignite emotional and physical intimacy at specific times during the process. The days need to remain in order, but there will likely be a week or so in between days. For instance, you may use fourteen weekends to progress through the fourteen activities. We recommend reading one day at a time, completing each day's activity before moving on to the next day. We understand this will be difficult for those of you who typically rush for the finish line aka climax. Slow down. Let us repeat. Slow down. The book is designed to be enjoyed. Small moments make for big finishes aka connections.

Throughout the pages ahead, you will see highlighted boxes called **Turnoffs.** The information provided in these boxes is intended to help you begin to identify what mistakes you might be making that put out the fire in your relationship. Turnoffs prevent connection and sabotage emotional and physical intimacy. These small, but significant errors in communication are unintentional. Turnoffs are meant to raise your awareness as partners and as a couple of what is working and what is not working in your attempts to connect.

Turnoffs prevent connection and sabotage emotional and physical intimacy.

The book is designed for all couples. The very nature of the book is to provide scaffolding for couples to create intimacy based on the uniqueness of their relationship. The sauciness of the activity is defined by the couple. It is our desire that couples will find *14 Days* meaningful multiple times in their lives. After all, having only one amazing experience is only a tease. The outcomes are endless based on time, emotional temperature, and level of investment in your relationship.

Trust us. Promise yourself and your partner to immerse yourself into these *14 Days of Foreplay* in an open-minded and optimistic way. We challenge you to launch into these intentional activities having faith that in 14 days, your relationship will be at a new and exciting level of connection that others are sure to notice. Have fun!

DAY #1:
Likes & Dislikes

Stripping Down:

Research indicates that one of the most important factors that highly satisfied couples possess is friendship. As with most of our friendships, knowing the little things about a person is critically important. No matter how long you have been with your partner, this activity asks you to get back to basics and interview one another to gain information about likes and dislikes. Do not assume you already know most of your spouse's favorites or pet peeves. These pitfalls of mind reading and making assumptions get couples into trouble. Assumptions block communication and lead us to forget that we are always evolving and changing. What may have been a tremendous dislike a few years ago may now only be a minor annoyance. Keep questioning, learning, and exploring your spouse's likes and dislikes, and you will communicate continued interest in who s/he is as a person.

Doing It:

The first step in this activity is for each spouse to independently complete an open-ended list of likes and dislikes. These lists are intended to ignite further questions and conversations.

Example:

Likes	Dislikes
warm towels	crumbs in the bed
hiking	golfing
showering together	lingerie
spaghetti	hot dogs
backyard bonfires	wet socks

After you have shared your list of likes and dislikes, develop your own unique list of five to ten questions to ask your spouse in interview style. Plan to spend at least twenty to thirty minutes going over each other's answers and additional questions.

Example:

1. What is your least desirable household chore?

2. What advice would you give to newlyweds?

3. How do you most like to spend Saturday mornings?

Remember to use the information you solicit! If you discover that your wife's secret craving is a Butterfinger candy bar, be mindful to pick one up at the convenience store the next time you stop for gasoline. Ladies, if you discover that your husband prefers to sleep with a fan on—you know what to do. Information is only useful when it is used. Put the information you learn into action. Be intentional.

"While a lot of it was common knowledge between us; there were a few revelations that we both smiled about."
- Christopher

Afterglow:

What surprises did you discover through this activity? How have your own responses changed over time? To establish accountabilities, talk with your spouse about ways that you will use the information you learned. Give your spouse some ideas about how to use the information exchanged—build a meaningful plan together.

TURNOFF:
assumptions

Assuming gets many couples into trouble, particularly in their sexual lives. *Catch yourself in the act of assuming* what your partner may be thinking or feeling and what she or he likes or dislikes. This is self-monitoring. *Actively stop the assumption* and gather evidence to verify that the information is accurate. Quite simply, *ask your partner* what s/he thinks about something rather than skipping this step. The process of checking in to gather information is often received as caring attentiveness. Your partner will know that you are genuinely interested in what s/he thinks, feels and has to say.

Day #1:
Likes & Dislikes

_____

_____

_____

_____

_____

_____

_____

_____

_____

_____

_____

DAY #2:
Taking Affection
on the Road

Stripping Down:

If you haven't figured it out by now, we believe that foreplay should, and does, begin long before entering the bed. For this activity, we are encouraging you to step out on the town. Although *what* you choose to do may seem important, actually, *how* you are together as a couple is most significant. Let people know you love your partner. This can be accomplished in many different ways.

Next time you are out, take notice of couple interactions. Look for cues that the members of a couple are really into one another. Signals that we often notice include lots of eye contact and gazing at one another. Of course, public display of affection (PDA) is the most obvious sign and comes in many forms. Hand-holding, putting an arm around the shoulder, and even a quick, playful swat on the rear are all ways of sending messages of "I love you" and "I want you." Smiling is perhaps the simplest way of showing affection toward your partner. A little grin can communicate happiness; add a sly wink, and you are now screaming friskiness! Some members of couples are able to block out all outside distractions and focus intently on their "dates." This communicates that you are most intrigued with who is right in front of you, not with what is all around you.

Doing It:

First you will need to determine what you will be doing and where you will be doing it for this activity's field trip. Tear a sheet of paper into ten pieces. Next, each of you will write down five ideas of what to do for this field trip. We encourage you to think of new and different ideas. Some popular ones that we hear often include going to the zoo, playing mini golf, taking a dancing lesson, scheduling a couple's massage, taking a cooking class, touring the local adult novelty shop, or getting matched tattoos. Okay, we don't often hear that last one, but wouldn't that be cool? After you have the ten playful date ideas written down, the elimination process begins. Go back and forth, each of you taking a turn to get rid of one idea at a time until you only have one remaining. You have come to a decision about your date!

Time for logistics. Choose a day and time to follow through with the plan. Decide now who will make the child-care arrangements if this needs to be done. We recommend that the partner who normally does this pass the torch to his or her partner to practice. Many times this is experienced as an act of affection or foreplay in and of itself. Don't underestimate this— initiating the call to a babysitter has an amazing way of communicating to your partner that he or she is special. In fact, take a moment right now to program the contact information for two babysitters into each of your phones. Now you can send a quick text to check availability on Wednesday morning when you are thinking about a hot date night for Friday night.

Launch mission PDA. Revisit the examples discussed earlier and even replicate what you see other couples doing that you like. It is the responsibility of each of you to make moves of affection toward your partner. Experiment with being subtle, tender, direct, and even provocative. (Just avoid getting arrested.)

Your goal for this date is to ignite the thought in an observer's mind, "They are so into each other." Usually, we advise people not to pay attention to what others may be thinking, but in this case, it helps to achieve the result of outwardly showing love and affection.

Afterglow:

What is your history of PDA as a couple? Has it always been part of your make-up? Was it stronger in the past as compared to the present? Is one of you less comfortable with these displays? If so, explore that discomfort verbally with your partner. Often, discomfort with displays of affection occurs because too much focus is being placed on what others might be thinking. Discover whether there are certain types of PDA that seem fun and playful to both of you. Remember, the more you practice these, the more natural and fulfilling they become.

"We were *that* couple! Steamy!" - Nicole

Day #2:
Taking Affection on the Road

DAY #3:
Touch Me Everywhere But There

Stripping Down:

Let us take you back to a time when you were sixteen, at the movie theatre, in the dark…and there was touching. Remember that amazing feeling of having your boyfriend/girlfriend touching you in the simplest ways and feeling nothing short of amazing? Why doesn't that occur in our marriages ten, twenty, thirty, forty, or fifty years later? There is plenty of research out there that tells us we won't ever feel this in our marriages because we have "evolved" or something clinically boring like that. It might be true that we won't be able to feel this way exactly or on most occasions in our marriages, due to a variety of factors, but we suggest that it is possible to re-create the tenth grade every once in a while in our marriages.

Often our sex lives within our marriages are focused on building up to intercourse. It seems that once we go there, we always go there. What about all of those amazing times in our lives when we didn't go there, and we had the times of our lives? Let's rewind and explore. We think you will be surprised what your fifteen-year-old self can do to enhance your adult self's sex life today!

Doing It:

Find a time when you and your spouse have a minimum of one hour alone. Rid yourselves of all distractions (cell phones, pets, etc.). This activity can be done with clothes on (for the authentic fifteen-year-old feel) or with clothes off (with the luxury of not being fifteen). Feel free to caress, kiss, stroke, etc., anywhere except for the genital areas. You can decide whether this includes breasts. Spend one hour exploring each other's bodies. Feel free to move your spouse's hand or lips to parts of your body that you want your partner to explore. Spend part of the time in silence, just focusing on your experience. Then you can quietly dialogue for the remainder of the time, describing what you are experiencing, what you want more or less of, and so on. Moans are welcomed, even encouraged.

Afterglow:

What did you like or dislike about this activity? Did it enhance your sexual relationship? If so, how? Would you make it part of your relationship on a regular basis? Were you surprised by anything that made you feel good? Was your spouse surprised by any of your physical expressions? Were you surprised by any of your spouse's physical expressions toward you? Did you experience an orgasm? If you did not, did you mind?

"Unexpectedly, this was my favorite day! Good thing moans were allowed!"
- Ann

Day #3:
Touch Me Everywhere But There

DAY #4:
I Choose You Because…

Stripping Down:

Marriage is a chosen relationship. It is different from being a son or daughter, a sister or brother, etc. When we get married, we explicitly choose a spouse. This is often done with considerable evaluation of this person's qualities. Early in a relationship, our reasons for choosing our spouses are easily in the forefront of our minds, and we are even able to vocalize these to our spouses on a fairly regular basis. For example, we might say, "I want to be with you because you make me laugh." But over time, we share these reasons for choosing one another less and less often. And when things become strained in a marriage, we could often use reminders of why we choose each other every day because we elect to stay married, and why we are committed to keeping the marriage strong.

Additionally, reminding ourselves of why we choose or chose our partners can often keep us from becoming frustrated by certain qualities. For example, you are irritated by your spouse's long decision-making process. It is helpful to recall that you chose him or her as a partner because you admired the person's ability to discern when making important decisions. You just might feel less frustrated.

Doing It:

Make a list of the reasons you "choose" your spouse. This exercise is about the here and now. Use present tense. Share these reasons with your spouse.

Examples: "I choose you because you believe in me."
"I choose you because we have shared dreams for our children."
"I choose you because you are kind to me and others."
"I choose you because I feel special and important around you."
"I choose you because you are always up for an adventure."

"This day was emotional for us. We said things we have never said before."
- Rebecca

Afterglow:

What did it feel like to recall the reasons you chose your partner originally, or why you choose your partner today? What did it feel like to express these thoughts and feelings with your spouse? Were you reminded of something you had forgotten? Did recalling these choices increase any patience or daily forgiveness in your marriage? Was your spouse surprised by any of your expressions?

TURNOFF:
invalidation

A common invalidating experience includes feeling unheard, ignored, and misunderstood. Therefore, to experience validation is to feel heard, acknowledged, understood, valued, soothed, and accepted. Validation comes in lots of different forms. It can be listening, a non-verbal sign of empathy such as a nod, asking clarifying questions to gain deeper understanding, or even a hug or gentle touch. Below are a number of validating phrases that we recommend you try on and experiment with.

Mmm

Aww.

Yeah.

That must hurt.

That's terrible.

I hear you.

That's a lot to deal with.

I can't imagine what you must be feeling.

I would feel the same way.

I can see you are really upset.

I'd feel _____ too (frustrated, sad, angry, confused, disappointed, nervous, etc.).

You look _____ (upset, shaken, fragile, etc.).

You seem a little _____ (troubled, concerned, worried, scared, sad, etc.).

That must really hurt.

I know just what you mean.

I can understand how you feel.

No wonder you are feeling _____.

Tell me more.

What happened next?

That must have really affected you.

How did you feel when...?

What bothers you the most about it?

Wow.

Neat.

Cool.

Excellent.

That's great.

That must have been exciting.

I can see why you are _____ (proud, afraid, sad, frustrated, annoyed, exhausted, etc.).

Day #4:
I Choose You Because...

_____

_____

_____

_____

_____

_____

_____

_____

_____

_____

_____

_____

DAY #5:
Pure Deliciousness

Stripping Down:

The Greek root, "aphrodisi," means "to love or desire." In mythology, we are all familiar with Aphrodite, the great Olympian goddess of beauty, love, pleasure, and procreation. Here we apply this sassy little root to bedroom desires and behaviors. An aphrodisiac is an agent such as a food or a drug that arouses sexual desire.

In order to be a true aphrodisiac, it has to create desire, not improve performance and ability, unlike pharmaceuticals. In this activity you and your partner will be searching for a spark to get things cooking in the bedroom (or kitchen).

A glance at historical reference and current fact finding generates a list of eighteen aphrodisiacs. Each food makes the list because of its shape or aroma or chemical basis. The food you eat may directly impact your sex life by affecting your hormones, brain chemistry, energy, and stress levels. Some foods actually increase circulation and blood flow to the genitals. Others are more psychologically suggestive because of shape or resemblance to sexual body parts.

*Aniseed*s, or "anise" seeds, when sucked, are believed to increase desire. Both aniseed and papaya are estrogenic, meaning that they have compounds that act like the female hormone, estrogen. Aniseed has been used as a folk remedy in promoting menstruation and milk production and in increasing female libido.

Avocados make the list due to their shape. Aztecs called the avocado tree a "testicle tree," as the fruit hangs in pairs, resembling male testicles. Grab some tortilla chips and enjoy some guacamole, but be careful not to get chip crumbs between the sheets.

Bananas are rich in potassium, magnesium, and B vitamins, which are claimed to be linked to sex hormone production. They also contain chelating minerals and the bromeliad enzyme, which are said to enhance the male libido. The phallic shape of the banana also shouldn't go unnoticed. We recommend dipping this fun fruit in chocolate sauce.

Chocolate has long been associated with love and is often gifted on dates, anniversaries, or romantic holidays, particularly Valentine's Day. It contains phenylethylamine and serotonin, known to be "feel good" chemicals.

Carrots were used by early Middle Eastern royalty to assist with seduction. The phallic shape of carrots is noted as part of their sexual charm.

Garlic increases blood flow and circulation, as it is filled with allicin. Stock the bedside table with mints and enjoy. Because of its reputation for igniting passions, Tibetan monks many years ago were not permitted in the monastery if they had been eating garlic.

Sweet basil is said to promote circulation with its scent, particularly impacting men. Historically, women would dust their breasts with sweet basil to drive men wild.

Chili peppers ignite body responses that mirror those experienced during a sexual encounter (sweating, rapid heart rate, and increased circulation). Feeling hot, hot, hot!

Figs make the list because they are said to resemble female sex organs.

Cucumbers have a scent believed to increase blood flow to a woman's vagina; again, these are phallic symbols.

Asparagus was famed as far back as the seventeenth century by Nicholas Culpepper, an English herbalist. Culpepper wrote that asparagus "stirs up lust." In nineteenth century France, bridegrooms were served three courses of asparagus prior to their weddings. Chemically, asparagus is a good source of fiber, vitamins A, B and C, potassium, thiamin, and folic acid. These components boost production of histamine, which is necessary for reaching orgasm in both men and women.

Almonds have long been viewed as symbols of fertility. The scent of almond has been thought by poets to arouse passion in females.

Oysters were identified in the second century by the Romans as an aphrodisiac. Okay, okay, so they resemble female genitalia too. However, they are also high in zinc, which has been linked to sexual potency (sperm) and libido in men. Raw oysters are best served with a glass of chilled champagne to ignite romance.

Pine nuts work in much the same way as oysters, as they, too, are high in zinc. They have been thought to stimulate libido since medieval times and have been used in the making of love potions for centuries.

Honey, drunk in a fermented form during medieval times, was said to promote sexual desire. In ancient Persia, couples enjoyed honey drinks called mead. They would drink mead every day for a month after they were married, in order to get into the right frame of mind for a successful marriage. This time period became known as the honeymoon. Honey contains vitamin B (needed for testosterone production) and boron (which helps the body metabolize and use estrogen).

Licorice has a smell that has been found to be particularly stimulating. It is even noted as having the ability to increase blood flow to the penis by 13 percent.

Ginger has been regarded as an aphrodisiac for centuries because of both its smell and its stimulation of the circulatory system.

Doing it:

Plan a meal or a picnic with a variety of the above mentioned sexually stimulating foods. Clothe yourselves in soft, free-flowing garments—or maybe just your bed sheets. Your senses will be ignited by texture, taste, scent, vision, and the sounds of moaning over such a sensual experience.

Afterglow:

What was most stimulating to your own senses? What was least stimulating? Do these aphrodisiacs offer clues to your sexuality and sense of eroticism? Do you need to add more chocolate to your sexual routine? Or garlic?

"I love preparing food for my wife. Now I can show her I love her and provoke eroticism."
- Neil

Day #5:
Pure Deliciousness

_____

_____

_____

_____

_____

_____

_____

_____

_____

_____

_____

_____

DAY #6:
PG-13, R, *or* X-Rated

Stripping Down:

Couples often struggle to verbally communicate their sexual desires or fantasies. This is not usually because they don't have any sexual desires or fantasies; more often, it is because they don't have a language for discussing them or they have never openly shared their sexual preferences. Therefore, doing so causes anxiety.

A sexual relationship results equally from your own desires, your partner's desires, and what you co-create together. Meeting one's own sexual needs with one's partner often builds more emotional and sexual intimacy between the members of a couple than if each partner was only focused on the other partner's sexual response. Traditionally, our culture focuses on telling our partners what they should do to pleasure us and how they should do it. This common message tells us two very unhelpful things: 1. We should know what to do to make our partners happy sexually, and 2. Our sexual relationships are about pleasing our partners and not about ourselves. Newsflash: Identifying your sexual preferences and communicating them is not selfish. It is an essential step in teaching your partner how to be his or her best partner to you.

A phenomenal sexual relationship results equally from your own desires, your partner's desire, and what you co-create together.

A nonthreatening way for members of a couple to begin to talk about their own sexuality with their partners is by simply doing a very old-fashioned pastime. Watch a movie together…with a twist.

Doing It:

Each partner chooses a movie that "turns him or her on." It may have a scene or two that is a turn-on, a relationship between characters that turns him or her on, a particular theme or time period that is a turn-on, etc. Avoid choosing a movie based solely on the physical attractiveness of an actor or actresses. Once you have chosen your movie, spend a seemingly simple evening with your spouse, watching the movie. While watching the movie, pause it and share with your spouse. Share what it is about a scene or element of the movie that feels sexy, erotic, or simply desirable for you. On a separate night, the other spouse shares his or her movie in the same fashion.

Afterglow:

What was the process of choosing a movie like for you? Was it easy? Was it difficult? Would your choice in a movie been different five years ago, ten years ago, or one year ago? What was it like telling your spouse which movie you chose? Did he or she already know that you found something about this film sexually arousing? What was the outcome of your sharing and discussion? What did you learn or gain as a married couple from this movie night? Are you hotter than the couple in the movies?

"Just reading about this activity, made my heart race. I was nervous to see what movie my partner chose. I was pleasantly surprised and even added it to my list of 'turn on" movies.' - Leigh

Day #6:
PG-13, R, or X-Rated

_____

_____

_____

_____

_____

_____

_____

_____

_____

_____

_____

_____

_____

DAY #7:
I Love *it* When…

Stripping Down:

Identifying moments in your marriage that not only feel good for yourself but also serve to build positive feelings *between* you and your spouse is important in learning to be intentional in thoughts and actions. This activity empowers individuals to play active roles in building positive feelings for themselves, their spouses, and for their marriages. In a sense, it is the mortar between the bricks in the foundation of a couple.

Doing It:

Slow down and take notice of moments in your marriage, moments that evoke positive feelings. When you have identified a behavior or connection between you and your spouse that feels positive, share this observation with your spouse by saying, "I love it when [insert observation here]."

Examples: "I love it when I walk into a room and I can smell your cologne."
"I love it when you answer my phone call with excitement in your voice."
"I love it when you text me to let me know you are thinking of me."
"I love it when you shower with me."
"I love it when we play soccer with the kids as a family."
"I love it when I see you laughing with your dad."

Afterglow:

What did it feel like to slow down and take note of moments that might otherwise have gone unobserved? What did it feel like to express these thoughts and feelings to your spouse? Were you surprised by anything that made you feel good? Was your spouse surprised by any of your expressions? Did you know that starting the coffee in the morning makes your partner want you?

"He says he feels loved when I ask him what makes him feel loved. He likes to know that he matters to me. Now I know to ask more often."
- Claire

Day #7:
I Love it When...

_____

_____

_____

_____

_____

_____

_____

_____

_____

_____

_____

_____

_____

DAY #8:
Dressing *the* Part

Stripping Down:

Physical intimacy is often short-changed due to our busy schedules. We all experience exhaustion when our lives collide with the thought, "We should have sex tonight." This often leads to rushed, predictable sex that checks the box. Whew, we can now say we are still the couple that has sex one or two times per week. The amount or frequency of sex is definitely secondary to the subjective feelings of satisfaction that result from the experiences. This is the old quantity versus quality debate taking shape in our sexual lives.

Now, don't misunderstand what is being said here. Spontaneous, quick sexual encounters can be very exciting. Often there is more lust and an animalistic feel that is quite stimulating. In this activity, however, the focus is not on how quickly climax is achieved but rather on setting the stage. The antici-pation of the big show is often the part that leads to a more satisfying experience.

The lead-up to the sexual encounter is key. Getting into the mindset can be assisted

> The anticipation of the big show is often the part that leads to a more satisfying experience.

by dressing the part. Wearing attire that is sensual or provocative is not only for the pleasure of one's partner but is also a way to feel more desirable. Scents of perfume and cologne are included in dressing.

Doing It:

Starting with the ladies, take an honest inventory of your lingerie selection. You don't necessarily need an arsenal of lace teddies; however, having one or two pieces that make you feel sexy may very well put your partner in the mood as well. Consider this your first layer of dressing.

Next to the top layer. A woman once spoke of her experience preparing for an anniversary date with her husband of fourteen years. She chose a slinky skirt and asked his opinion about what top would go best with the skirt. She received a lukewarm response from her husband, which surprised and hurt her in the moment. As they talked, she learned that he was more turned on by a pair of jeans than by something more formal and flirty. This is a good reminder about the pitfall of making assumptions about what your partner likes or doesn't like. Even with the "first layer" suggested above, you may find that your partner isn't necessarily drooling over lingerie. Don't take this personally; it's usually just the spouse's own personal preference. For this top layer, it is recommended to talk with your partner and ask directly what he or she enjoys seeing you wear. A shopping trip where your partner picks out items for you to consider wearing may be fun.

The final layer for the ladies includes scents and accessories. Apply a sensual perfume to your pulse points. These are the areas on your body where the blood vessels are closest to the skin and where heat emanates. Some application spots include inner wrists, the base of the throat, behind the earlobes, in the cleavage, behind the knees, and inside the elbows. Don't rub the perfume into your skin; this changes the chemistry. Finishing accessory touches may be a fabulous pair of stilettos or jewelry that your partner has gifted to you in the past.

For the man in the relationship, be mindful of what works for your partner. If the sporty look tickles her fancy, go with tear away pants and baseball hat. If she would lose it over seeing you in an Oxford button-down with a sport coat, make it happen. Don't feel pressure to guess what would work for her; just ask her. Your willingness to take her suggestion may be a surprising tool in your foreplay playbook. Remember this!

Again, think about dressing in layers. When putting this daily activity to the foreplay test, be mindful about each step along the way from choosing your underwear (boxers, briefs, boxer-briefs, or commando?) to remembering the cologne. She will feel special if you take extra steps to ready yourself for time with her.

Afterglow:

What decisions did you make about dressing with the foreplay mindset that was either new or surprising to you? How did you feel as you were readying yourself? If you chose to consult with your partner ahead of time, what was that experience like? What would you say is an essential part of your dressing as foreplay? What worked for you that your partner did or wore? What will you try differently for next time?

"We were turned on before we even left the store!"
– Susan

TURNOFF:
inner critic

Often the inner critic shows up when we are purchasing or wearing clothing. Body image concerns will sneak up on you and take away from moments of feeling sexy and desirable and yearning for a physical touch. Acknowledge your inner critic and its voice, but then gently let your critic know that there is no room for it in your moment. You have authority over your thoughts and feelings. Decide what you will think and how you will feel.

Day #8:
Dressing the Part

_____

_____

_____

_____

_____

_____

_____

_____

_____

_____

_____

_____

DAY #9:
Play Hard

Stripping Down:

"All work and no play makes Jack a dull boy." Scratch that; all work and no play makes a dull relationship! Why work hard at a marriage if the marriage isn't fun? In couples' therapy, we often ask a couple to tell us what is fun about their marriage, and all too often, they are at a loss for words. They can say how they pay the bills, run the kids to soccer and guitar practice, attend local charity events, and even how they climb the corporate ladder, but often couples can't tell us how to play! Having fun in a marriage is a great way to add to the marital "bank account" so that when life gets hard and takes "withdrawals," you have plenty to borrow on. Additionally, a person is more willing to work on the marriage because they are eager to get back to "playing hard."

Doing It:

What do you do for fun? What would you do for fun? (Together!) Rock concerts? Yoga? Running? Book readings at the local library? Sci-fi movies? Online gaming? Rock climbing? Attending local sporting events? Hosting parties? Trying a new restaurant? It is important to remember that each of you may define "fun" or "play" differently. For this particular day, seek out an activity that has mutual buy-in. In short, you both have to want to try it because it sounds fun. There are times when a bit of personal sacrifice in a relationship is a gift. For example, a husband might find gardening to be wonderfully fun and enjoyable. His wife on the other hand does not have playing in the dirt on her list of "fun". She may join the activity of gardening benevolently as a gift of togetherness to her husband. Although this gesture is awesome and encouraged, it is not for today. This day is to be co-created, considering what would be experienced as fun, exciting, and playful for both partners. Mud volleyball?

Have a conversation with your spouse about what you already do that is fun or what you want to try to do that might be fun. And then do it. *Play hard.*

Afterglow:

What did it feel like to play hard? What was it about playing that felt good? How can you make this happen more in your marriage? Make a plan for how to fit this into your lives. Can you do it weekly? Monthly? What would it take to make it happen? Babysitters? Budgeting? How do you think committing to playing hard will strengthen your marriage?

"We went to this community Easter Egg Hunt. I thought it would be lame. But as we were racing through the open field, it began to rain. We stopped and kissed each other. I thought I would explode. I can't remember the last time we kissed like that." - David

Day #9:
Play Hard

_____

_____

_____

_____

_____

_____

_____

_____

_____

_____

_____

_____

DAY #10:
Take *a* Peek

Stripping Down:

This day will draw your eyes to yourself and, with reflection and sharing, will draw your eyes and your spouse's eyes to one another. Often we have ideas of how we see ourselves, ideas of how our spouses see us, and ideas of how others, outside of our marriages, see us. That is a whole lot of seeing! Looking at the similarities and differences in these perceptions can lead to interesting insights into behaviors within our relationships.

For example, if you see yourself as independent but think that your spouse sees you as stubborn, this perception will influence your behavior. Another example might be that you think others, outside of your marriage, perceive you as organized and ambitious, but you describe yourself as overwhelmed and desiring more free time in your life.

Sharing these "peeks" with your spouse helps the two of you to build knowledge about one another and sensitivities to ways to behave with and understand each other. This might lead to an increase in appreciation, patience, and curiosity for yourself and/or for your spouse.

Doing It:

Each of you make three lists:

4. How I see me

5. How my spouse sees me

6. How others see me

Share these lists with one another.

Afterglow:

Process with one another. What did you see when you took a peek? Were there perceptions that you were surprised by? Disagreed with? Agreed on? What did you learn or gain as a married couple from these peeks?

"He actually thinks I'm funny! I always thought he was just humoring me. And earlier I learned that my laugh turns him on. It's a win all around!" - Michael

Day #10:
Take a Peek

_____

_____

_____

_____

_____

_____

_____

_____

_____

_____

_____

_____

DAY #11:
Let's Get Wet

Stripping Down:

Brace yourselves. We are about to use the word lubrication way too many times. Lubrication makes just about everything smoother and, dare we say, more fun. However, a lack of natural lubrication produced by a woman should *not* be considered indicative of a lack of arousal. There are many physiological factors that can contribute to an absence or a diminished amount of naturally produced lubrication. The point is, natural or not, slick and slippery is ideal. Whether your body naturally produces enough or you have to supplement it with your choice of artificial lubrication, it matters not.

Playing with water, oil, non-petroleum-based lubricants, lotions, lathered soap, etc., will enhance your sexual experience. Play not only in or with genital areas, but use the largest sex organ you have: your skin. The sense of touch is erotic, sensual, and intimate.

Doing It:

Decide on one of the following, or try all three!

1. Take a bath or shower together. Take the time to feel your partner's body with the aid of the water and soap. Wash each other's bodies. Kiss. Caress. Explore. Try all of this with your eyes closed. With your eyes open.

2. Take a dip in the pool or hot tub. Take the time to feel your partner's body with the aid of the water. Hold one another in the water. Play with the Jacuzzi jets. Kiss. Caress. Explore.

3. Choose a comfortable location, perhaps the bedroom, to play with lotion or oil. Take the time to feel your partner's body with the aid of the lotion or oil. Kiss. Caress. Explore. Slide. Experiment with pressure (lightly touching or more firmly caressing and rubbing).

Afterglow:

In what ways did water or lubrication add excitement or arousal to your foreplay? In what ways did it deter from arousal?

"Sensual and freeing."
- Genevieve

Day #11:
Let's Get Wet

_____

_____

_____

_____

_____

_____

_____

_____

_____

_____

_____

_____

DAY #12:
Foreplaying 101—
The Playbook

Stripping Down:

We are creatures of habit and routine. This applies to most areas of our lives. We tend to drive the same routes to work, cook the same four to six meals, and even wash our bodies in highly predictable sequences in the shower. Examining our "playbooks" has great potential for increasing satisfaction in our sex lives and beyond. By "playbook," we are referring to the maneuvers and techniques that a couple uses in the initial stages of intimate connection. As with other areas, it is fun, and perhaps a little unnerving, to hear new ideas. We encourage you both to keep an open mind when reading over some of the suggestions offered here. You chose to read this book because you are searching for greater connection with your partner. Hopefully you will find that that connection results because of the journey, not the destination.

Men are like microwaves, and women are like slow cookers. There are certainly times when "quickies" suit the situation. We would venture a guess, however, that what would be preferable would be an intentional foreplay adventure to tend to both the emotional and the physical needs. A bit more focused time and attention may be needed to adequately arouse the female member of a couple. (Remember—slow cooker). Physical arousal mechanisms for males and females are similar and involve increasing the blood flow to sexual organs. For women, this involves lubrication, which, along with erect nipples, is a sign of arousal. Let's begin.

Lesson 1: Start foreplay outside of the bedroom. Begin with a compliment and lots of eye contact. Some nonsexual touching is encouraged. Nonsexual touching refers to rubbing shoulders, caressing the small of his or her back, and even locking hands.

Lesson 2: Set the stage by incorporating scents and sounds. These may enhance the experience and lead to it lasting longer.

Lesson 3: Build anticipation. Take time before undressing. Allow hands to wander over the body, over the clothes. Do not go immediately for the hot spots.

Lesson 4: Lights on. :)

Lesson 5: Gentle and tender wins out over rough and quick (at least to start with).

Lesson 6: Use provocative talk (we prefer this term to "dirty talk") and messages of love (compliments). Moaning and other sensual noises are encouraged, as they are great feedback nuggets when you like something that is happening.

Lesson 7: Explore all parts of each other's bodies, not just the sexual ones. It is common to go directly (and solely) for the breasts, vagina, and penis. Mix it up by visiting calves, stomach, earlobes, feet, and rear ends.

Lesson 8: Give feedback to your partner. Communication during foreplay and physical intimacy can come in the form of sensual noises, directives/instructions, moving your partner's mouth or hands to pleasing parts, or encouraging his/her body into positions to try different acts. Don't hesitate to ask for what you want! Remember, your partner wants to please you; help him/her out.

Lesson 9: Role-play. The simplest form of role-playing is dominant/submissive. These are more extreme words to highlight the arrangement where one person initiates and takes over. One of you is in control, and the other simply complies with requests. It is intended to be fun—not a power and control nightmare.

Lesson 10: Props are fair game. The use of feathers, vibrators, bullets, clamps, ties, plugs, and of course, lingerie, should be considered a fun way to add a little variety and spice. Keep in mind toys are not intended to be a replacement for or insult to your partner. Rather, they should be viewed as supplements to any well-rounded sex life.

Lesson 11: Visit downtown. We don't mean skyscrapers.

Lesson 12: Slippery when wet. Lubrication is not optional, but essential. It heightens pleasure and allows for ease of entry.

Lesson 13: Try new things. Begin with a bath or shower together, massage one another with oils, or bring some yumminess into the bedroom. (Chocolate-covered strawberries or flavored syrups are a couple of ideas to get you thinking. Ooh, don't forget to try whipped cream!)

Doing It:

Identify your current playbook. Write down the foreplay techniques that you use now or have used in the past. Be specific. Although it may feel awkward to talk openly about these parts of your sex life, it will help to share common language with your partner. Communicating will move you both to the same page.

Now, work on revising the playbook. Add intriguing "plays" that you may have been thinking or fantasizing about for a while. Agree to eliminate plays that are no longer effective. Talk about what plays to practice that may increase "wins" for you as a couple. You may experience surprises about what your partner identifies as fun or important. Try ranking, in order of enjoyment, the plays on your foreplay list.

"We added music and role-playing. I wonder why we never thought to do this before." - Steven

Afterglow:

Now it is time to practice. Go and *do*. Remember to have fun and experiment.

TURNOFF:
lack of freedom to laugh

Often when we are trying something new, we feel awkward and at times even fumble through the moment. This type of experience can easily be weathered by laughter. Permission to laugh and be awkward will build intimacy and will allow you to take more risks with yourself and with each other.

Day #12:
Foreplaying 101—The Playbook

DAY #13:
Be Schooled

Stripping Down:

Day twelve gave you the opportunity to assess what you already know and do and gave you permission to do more of what you already know but were maybe hesitant to do. This activity invites you to go one step further in your exploration of physical foreplay and the physical act of sex.

Learning is a lifetime pursuit and will only serve you for the better. This is true about sexual knowledge. Often individuals feel that they should know it all already, and if they don't know something, they feel inadequate, as if their time to learn it has passed. Additionally, there are individuals who were schooled about sex in less than credible arenas such as the public school bus. Can you imagine the possibilities that would open up to you and your relationship if you learned about sex and physical foreplay with intention and from credible sources? You are about to find out!

Doing It:

Visit the library or bookstore. Seek out books that focus on physical foreplay and the act of sex. A book with illustrations would be best. There are classics like *The Joy of Sex* and the *Kama Sutra* and there are more modern reads such as *Sex for Dummies* and *Discovering Your Couple Sexual Style*. Other good reads are *The Guide to Getting It On* and *For Yourself: The fulfillment of Female Sexuality*. A scan of the bookshelves will provide a host of reading resources on positions and general knowledge of the human body and sexual function. All of these will be helpful for this day.

Now, have a study session. Read. Discuss. Giggle. Practice. Review.

Afterglow:
What new information or ideas did you learn in your study session? What misguided sexual knowledge did you unlearn?

"It felt so normal to know that we were not the only ones who didn't measure up to what we see in the movies. And what I learned on the school bus IS NOT TRUE." - Sean

Day #13:
Be Schooled

_____

_____

_____

_____

_____

_____

_____

_____

_____

_____

_____

_____

_____

DAY #14:
Vows

Stripping down:

A wedding day is a kickoff event for a marriage. It is meant to celebrate two people's decision to commit to one another. An important and traditional ritual embedded within every wedding ceremony is the recital of vows. By definition, a vow is a promise or an oath. Typical wedding vows express a commitment to stick by your partner in both the best of times and the worst. An example of a traditional wedding vow follows.

"I, Bride/Groom, take you, Groom/Bride, to be my wife/husband, to have and to hold from this day forward, for better or for worse, for richer, for poorer, in sickness and in health, to love and to cherish, from this day forward until death do us part."

Today you are being asked to create a different set of vows—marriage vows. Wedding vows tend to be general and abstract. In contrast, marriage vows are specific and practical. They should have utility. They should weave together emotions, promises, expectations, needs, and commitment.

Consider your marriage vows a constitution of sorts. The Constitution

> Marriage vows are specific and practical. They should have utility.

of the United States was created to be a guide, provide structure, define limits, and perhaps most importantly, allow for change by way of the amendment process. A country and a couple have in common the fact that they are both "systems." Systems are dynamic and evolving, requiring that the "rules" that govern them are not rigid and that the members of the system can be flexible to amend them as needed.

Doing It:

The process of coming together to discuss and capture what you promise to one another can often be just as strengthening as the outcome of the written vows. After the drafts have been filtered through and narrowed down, type up the final copy of your vows and sign it as if it is a binding contract. This act symbolically brings with it a sense of accountability. Next, take turns reading your vows to each other, verbally making the promises a living, active commitment. Practice looking each other in the eyes during the recital. Speak slowly and meaningfully, punctuating important points through tone or touch. Hold hands during the recital, and don't forget to seal the process with a kiss, just as you did on your wedding day.

Afterglow:

Process with one another the best part of this day for you. What was it like to think about vows in this way? How did you feel, creating your vows together? How would they have been different if they had been constructed individually? (If you believe this might have value, engage in this process at a later time.) How did reciting these vows feel similar or different from your wedding vows?

"Our marriage has changed so much over the last 30 years. It was beautiful to talk about our past and our future in such an intentional way."
- Jean

Day #14:
Vows

_____

_____

_____

_____

_____

_____

_____

_____

_____

_____

_____

_____

_____

Where Did *all this* Foreplay Lead You?

You were courageous enough to play and explore; now, how does this translate into the benefits of intention and lifelong intimacy? What will day fifteen, sixteen, one hundred, or one thousand look like for your relationship?

We imagine that when you chose to read this book, you had expectations of a recipe for amazing sex, deep intimacy, and a passionate relationship. So, are you having amazing sex and deeper emotional intimacy, and is your relationship more passionate than it was before the experience of *14 Days*? We imagine that your relationship is well on its way.

It is our hope that doing these 14 days invited you to bring new gestures of intention into your relationship. By taking risks and showing vulnerability, you created intimacy. You increased trust and communication, and you intentionally made your relationship a priority. You decided that play is important and valuable. Who knew that playing

Who knew that playing with bananas, dressing up in blue jeans, taking a shower together, and expressing future dreams were all equally important foreplays to intimate relationships?

with bananas, dressing up in blue jeans, taking a shower together, and expressing future dreams were all equally important foreplays to intimate relationships?

Gestures of intention are essential to ongoing health of your intimate relationship. They will serve as valuable tools for all experiences in your relationship including problem solving, expressing emotion, and coping with change, loss, or trauma. They will serve as tools for embracing the joys and triumphs that life will bring to you. They will be tools for expressing new and changing wants and desires and for knowing how to listen and turn toward one another even when your instincts are to turn away. You have invested in your future.

The activities provided you with the courage and trust to have a more deeply intimate relationship for a lifetime. You have created a book of plays that you can and *should* come back to again and again. Each time you "run a play" you will learn something new, and you may even run the play a little differently, over time. If so, this is most certainly evidence that your playbook *is and has been* working over the years.

Ready *to* Go Again?

Now that you are flying high on *14 Days of Foreplay*, let's keep it going! Would you be willing to share your experience of these *14 Days* with others? Would you be interested in teaching others what worked and what didn't work about your *14 Days* and perhaps even sharing your ideas for a Day 15? Please consider inspiring other couples to play by visiting us on the web at **www.14daysforeplay.com**.

Made in the USA
San Bernardino, CA
23 June 2014